Thankful Me Using My ABCs

Terrie Sizemore

Thankful Me Using My ABCs

This is a work of fiction.

Text and Illustrations copyrighted

by Terrie Sizemore ©2023

Library of Congress Control Number: 2022912473

All rights reserved. No part of this book may be

reproduced, transmitted, or stored in an information retrieval

system in any form or by any means,

graphic, electronic, or mechanical without prior written

permission from the author.

Printed in the United States of America

A 2 Z Press LLC

PO Box 582

Deleon Springs, FL 32130

bestlittleonlinebookstore.com

sizemore3630@aol.com

440-241-3126

ISBN: 978-1-946908-68-1

Dedication:

This book is dedicated
to the God I love
and to
all my friends who
make me thankful
each and every day.

I'm so glad you've joined me today.
Do read on, this is only the start.
For the many things to be thankful for
that make us smile and bless our hearts.
Let me share all the things important to me,
And I'll do this by using my ABC's!

'A' is for how I appreciate the alphabet and art,
All the ripe avocados and sweet apples in a tart.
For awesome astronauts, and athletes accepting what is fair,
and aloe vera that soothes my skin in August's warm air.

'B' for birthdays and bright blue balloons, banana splits and bees,
Blueberries and baseball, breakfast, and birds high in the trees.
I'm thankful too for bunny rabbits, baskets, books, and beauty,
And all brave friends who stand up for others and do their duty.

C 'C' is eating candy round the campfire with my cousins and their cats,
Cosmic colored crayons and clumsy clowns in funny hats,
Celery and carrots, cakes and cookies that we share,
Cheerful clothes and Christmas when we show how much we care.

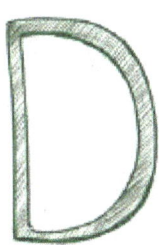
'D' makes me thankful for days of the week, didgeridoos, and drums,
Dogs, dads, dumplings, dragonflies, and donuts in our tums!
Daffodils and daisies and for dates we should remember,
After Thanksgiving, we love Christmas which delights us each December.

E 'E' for everyday I'm grateful for my eyebrows, ears, and eyes,
For the eggs we hunt at Easter and the eagles in the skies.
For elephants and echoes, elves, and engines in our cars,
Electric and elastic, elbows, and Eskimo ice-cream bars!

'F' for how fortunate I am enjoying freedom, faith, and fun,
A fort down on the farm to build and fields through which to run.
Fantastic flowers, funny frogs, fresh air, and flashing fish,
For family and friends who all share my French fries in a big dish.

'G' is for giggling, goldfish, gloves, and games, giraffes and gruff goats,
I'm thankful for guitars to strum, gorillas, grass, and gravy boats.
Geese and gum, gymnastics, green grapes piled up by the plateful,
The gentle love of grandmama and grandpa always makes me grateful.

'H' for hugs that make me happy, handkerchiefs, and holidays,
Hummingbirds that hover and the handsome horse who neighs.
Hijinks as my hat's hurled by the breeze from off my head,
I missed it with my hands, but Hooray! the hedge caught it instead!

'I' makes me thankful for insects, infants, incredible imagination, and igloos made of ice - all these deserve appreciation! Islands, ice cream, inks, and imps, night-time illuminations, Iguanas and the iris flowers, inspiring Springtime indications.

'J' brings joy for January, jubilations, and jokes in July and June,
Juggling, jumping, jellybeans, and eating jam straight from the spoon.
Journeys as we jabber, jungles, jewels, jazzy jets, and jade,
Jars of sweets on Halloween, Jack-O-Lanterns that we made.

K 'K' is for kangaroos, koalas, kiwis, kittens, kites, and kings,
K-9's in kennels, shoelace knots, and the bright kookaburra's wings.
My mom who knew the knack to mend my grazed knee comes to mind,
As kneeling there she kissed my tears, so knowledgeable and kind.

'L' is how we're so lucky living lives so full of laughter and love,
Lifeguards, landmarks, lightning, lighthouse lanterns up above.
Ladybirds on leaves and lobsters deep down in the sea,
Learning lots in libraries, I like when Dad sings lullabies to me.

M 'M' makes me merry for macaroni, muffins, milkshakes, and May,
Maracas, mariachi music, melodies of songs we love to play.
Marshmallows at our picnic as wait for the midnight moon,
Majestic meatballs shaped like meteorites as we make
many memorable moments to the tunes.

N 'N' for nature makes me thankful for the newts and nightingales,
For nests and nectar, nanny goats, and noble old 'nar-whales.'
For noodles, neighbors, night-time, naps, and numbers nought to nine,
Ninjas, noses, nurseries, and necklaces that shine.

'O' is for orange October pumpkins carved with oval open mouths,
And okra in the gumbo that they cook down in the South.
Ostriches and orchids, wise old owls, and this mighty ox,
Olives, onions, oregano, and deep-sea ocean rocks.

P 'P' for pink piglets and pug pups in packs, peacocks, and panda play.
For pudding, peach and pumpkin pie, and pizzas our favorite way!
Poppies, pansies, paper, precious photographs in books,
Pajamas, pancakes, and pillows piled in peaceful reading nooks.

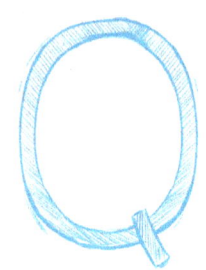

'Q' has me appreciating quiet time under Queen-sized comfy quilts,
The quirky, quickstep quiver when I first tried out some stilts.
Quavers, quartets, quizzes, questions, quiches, quills if I please.
It's quite a queue of qualities - I give thanks for all of these!

'R' - I love reading and relaxing in a robe while I recline,
Seeing the rainbow rising proudly after rain in bright sunshine.
For roosters, rhinos, robins, root beer, raisins, ribbons, rice,
Rodeos and rollercoasters and raspberry recipes oh-so-nice!

 'S' for sharing stories and singing songs from sunrise to sunset,
Swimming in the sparkling sea, we splash and get so wet.
Sitting seeing shooting stars in my sweatshirt, scarf, and shoes,
I'm thankful snuggled safe and sound and slowly start to snooze.

T 'T' makes me so thankful for tantalizing taco toppings, tortoises, and trees,
And thanks for tuneful trombone tones transported on the breeze.
For Tuesdays, Thursdays, trucks and toys, for teachers short and tall,
Telephones, tomatoes, tents: I'm thankful for them all!

'U' is for the spiky urchin underdog and the unique unicorn,
He's unicycling upside-down and balanced on his horn!
Ukeleles, uncles, and this unlimited universe,
I'm thankful for umbrellas when the rain is getting worse!

'V' for vegetables and vitamins that are very vital in my view,
Valuable and virtuous Victor, vibrant, valiant, and true.
Village veterinarians in vans, volcanos, and victories to rejoice,
Vacations, villas, valleys, verbs, and vowels all in my voice!

W 'W' - the wonderous world around us, wide wilderness I want to know.
Winter's white and is a wonderland of weightless wisps of snow.
Water, wind, and waffles, woolly coats to wrap up warm,
Each weekday wholesome thankful wishes within begin to form.

'X' - I love the sound of wooden blocks that sing on xylophones.
I'm grateful for the x-rays that help doctors check my bones.
For 'x's' and 'o's' on my card that says, 'Forget me not,'
X makes me appreciate the eXciting things I've got!

Y 'Y' In the yard we've yelled and yodeled, then a sleepy bedtime yawn,
Yippee! The night yields to the bright and yellow sun at dawn.
There's yachts and yo-yos, yoga, yolks, and yaks down at the zoo,
But one thing I'm most grateful for in all of this is you!

Z

'Z' - I'm grateful in my garden with zucchini and my lemon zest,
For kites that zig zag as the zephyr wind blows from the west.
For zookeepers and zebras and zeppelins up in the sky,
And for the zipper on my raincoat as it keeps me warm and dry!

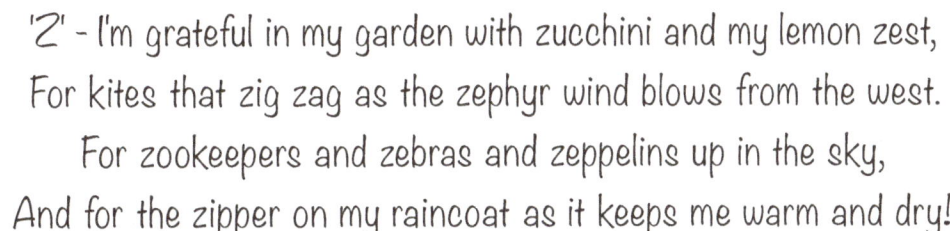

There's all twenty-six letters here from A right through to Z,
My ABCs of thankfulness I've shared for you from me.
But there are so many wonders in the world that lift my mood,
A thousand pages more might fully cover all my gratitude!

I'm thankful for almonds, ants, baboons and braids, chickens, cloaks, and clocks,
Donkeys digging emeralds and especially energetic frantic frocks!
And a great ginormous hippo holds such an impressive invention,
Janitors in jackets, Oh my, there's just too much to mention!

Kumquats, keyboards, ketchup, and the whistling of a kettle,
Leopards, lipstick, magic markers, machines made out of metal,
Nuns and notebooks, old oak trees, Olympics, ointment, paint,
Perky paws on pets and quests for quarters old and quaint.

Roaring rapids, stripy socks, tall tales of tangled thread,
For umpteen pairs of underwear, words unselfish and unsaid.
For vacuums, vows, and vehicles, for vests and violins,
Whistles, wheels, and windmills, wanderlust and little wins.

Things that have the 'X-factor,' youth and yesterday,
Zany zooming with my friends, I'm zapped from all the play.
Find things to be thankful for, each and every day.
Let thankful come out in all you do and say!

Because, you see, there's just so much around us that delights,
That makes me thankful for the many glorious sounds and sights!
Be thankful with your ABCs and take joy in who you are.
Make gratitude your attitude and you are sure to go so far.

'B' Thankful!

A_____
B_____
C_____
D_____
E_____
F_____
G_____
H_____
I_____
J_____
K_____
L_____
M_____
N_____
O_____
P_____
Q_____
R_____
S_____
T_____
U_____
V_____
W_____
XYZ_____

www.ingramcontent.com/pod-product-compliance
Lightning Source LLC
Chambersburg PA
CBHW042015120526
44592CB00043B/2898